BE CREATIVE

Bedroom
Makeover

Anna Claybourne

A+
Smart Apple Media

Published by Smart Apple Media,
an imprint of Black Rabbit Books
P.O. Box 3263, Mankato, Minnesota 56002
www.blackrabbitbooks.com

Printed in the United States of America at Corporate Graphics, North Mankato, Minnesota.

Published by arrangement with the Watts Publishing Group LTD, London.

Library of Congress Cataloging-in-Publication Data
Claybourne, Anna.
 Bedroom makeover / Anna Claybourne.
    pages cm -- (Be creative)
 Includes index.
 Summary: "Using clear, illustrated step-by-step directions, this book explains how to create fun accessories and decorations for the bedroom with bits of fabric, ribbon, buttons, and more. Basic sewing skills are taught, and ideas for other crafts are prompted. Equipment resources and glossary are included"
--Provided by publisher.
 ISBN 978-1-59920-695-0 (library binding)
 1. Sewing--Juvenile literature. 2. Textile crafts--Juvenile literature.
 3. Bedrooms--Juvenile literature. 4. Children's rooms--Juvenile literature. I. Title.
 TT712.C59 2013
 646.204--dc23

                                                      2011053503

Produced for Franklin Watts by White-Thomson Publishing

Author: **Anna Claybourne**
Project manager: **Rachel Minay**
Creative director: **Simon Balley**
Design: **Balley Design Limited**
Designer/Illustrator: **Andrew Li**

Picture Credits
aboikis 23, AKaiser 24/25, Alaettin YILDIRIM 4–5/16–17, Alena Ozerova 11, Ana Vasileva 4/12/13, Andrea Slatter 29, Aprilphoto 2/26/30, AVAVA 5, Baloncici 12/13, Crystal Kirk 18, Dmitry Melnikov 2/4/30–31/32, Ed Phillips 2/4/20/21/30, Elena Elisseeva 25, Elena Schweitzer 12/14/18/21, ericlefrancais 26, J. Broadwater 13, Jiri Hera 13/14/32, karam Miri front cover/2/3/5/10/11/13/18/30–31, Karkas 4/13, Kayros Studio "Be Happy!" 13, Kimberly Hall 3/5/8/14/16/18/20/31/32, Madlen 27/28, marymary 3/4/5/6/12/13/22/23/30/31, Masterov Egor 28, Monkey Business Images front cover/19/23, Morozova Oxana 19, Nataliia Melnychuk 18, NatesPics 21, Nattika 3/4/10/17, newyear2008 14/15, Olga K front cover/5/8/9/16/17, qingqing 7, R. Cherubin 28/29, Ramon Berk 29, Razvy 13, Roman Peregontsev front cover/5/8/9/16/17, ronstik 22, Solar 23, Steve Cukrov 3/27/31/32/back cover, STILLFX 27, trekandshoot 29, Tupungato 29, vnlit 29, wacpan 27.

PO1435
2-2012

9 8 7 6 5 4 3 2 1

Contents

Words in **bold** are in the glossary on page 31.

Creative Thinking

It's time to get creative! More and more people are making, crafting, and designing their own stuff. It's satisfying and fun to do, and it means that you can have things that no one else has. It saves you money too! If you really enjoy it, you could even end up designing or making things for a living.

Get the Gear!

The projects in this book mostly use sewing and craft materials such as card stock, glue, felt, fabric, thread, pins, needles, ribbons, and buttons. You may have a lot of these at home anyway. If not, there's an equipment guide on page 30 to show you where you can find them.

A Room of Your Own

Your bedroom is your own place, where you can chill out with friends, read, chat, or spend time on hobbies. Use the projects in this book to stamp your own style on your space—as well as making it more cozy and comfy.

Safety

Remember to keep strings, cords, and sharp things like pins, needles, and scissors away from small children.

Tip!
You don't have to follow all the projects exactly. If you like, you can use the ideas and methods in this book to come up with your own original creations.

Reuse and Recycle

Crafting can help to save the planet! For many of the projects in this book, you can reuse old clothes, fabrics, cards, and other things instead of buying new stuff that uses up the earth's resources or sending old stuff to the landfill.

Tip!
If you have a sewing machine and know how it works, you can use it for some of the projects in this book.

Little Birds

These cute birds are easy to make. Hang them on your window frame, wall, or bed.

Get the Gear!

- Tracing paper and pencil
- 2 pieces of felt fabric, about 5 inches (12 cm) square
- Scissors, pins, and needles
- Colorful strong thread or **embroidery** thread
- Tape measure or ruler
- About 4 inches (10 cm) of thin ribbon or yarn
- Handful of toy stuffing (from a craft shop)—or you can use a wad of yarn
- 2 buttons or beads for eyes

1 Trace this bird shape onto tracing paper, and cut it out.

2 Lay your two pieces of felt one on top of the other, and pin the paper shape on top. Then cut around the shape, through both layers of felt. Take off the pins and paper.

3 Make your piece of ribbon or yarn into a loop and put it between the felt pieces, as shown. Pin the two pieces together, leaving enough space to sew around the edge of the bird.

4 Thread your needle and tie a knot at the end. Sew around the edge of the bird, using a **running stitch** (see box below). Sew about ¼ in. (0.5 cm) in from the edge. Make sure you also sew through the loop to hold it in place.

5 When you're nearly all the way around, stop sewing and leave a gap about 1 in. (2 cm) wide. Remove the pins. Poke in some toy stuffing or yarn. Finish sewing along the gap, knot the thread, and snip it off.

6 Finish off by sewing on two small buttons or beads for eyes (see box on page 13).

How to Do a Running Stitch

A running stitch is a very simple stitch where you simply sew in and out of the fabric in a straight line. It is most useful for sewing thick fabrics, to **gather** fabrics, or to make a decorative stitch.

Tip!
If you're hanging your bird up high, or need to put in a hook or nail to hang it from, ask an adult to help.

Bedroom Bunting

In the past, **bunting** was just used for fairs and street parties. But now indoor bunting is a big trend. String it up to decorate your room—you can make it any color or pattern you like.

Get the Gear!

- 1 big piece of fabric (felt or fleece is recommended) or several smaller pieces of different colors or patterns
- About 3–5 yd. (3–5 m) of ribbon or **bias tape** about 1 in. (2 cm) wide
- Tape measure and scissors
- Pins, needles, and thread

1 Bunting flags can be large or small, but a good size is about 4 in. (10 cm) wide at the base and 6 in. (15 cm) long. To make a flag, measure and cut out a triangle-shaped piece of fabric.

4 in. (10 cm)

6 in. (15 cm)

Tip!
Cut triangles like this to avoid wasting any fabric.

2 For each yard or meter of ribbon you will need about 4 flags. So for 3 yd. (3 m) of ribbon, you will need 12 flags.

1 yd. (1 m)

Safety

Keep bunting away from young children and babies. Ask an adult to help you hang it up safely so that it can't fall down.

3 Lay your ribbon flat and arrange the flags along it, one every 10 in. (25 cm).

10 in. (25 cm)

4 Fold the ribbon over so it covers the wide end of each triangle, and pin through all three layers.

5 Then sew along the pinned line using a **backstitch** (see box below), removing the pins as you go.

How to Do a Backstitch

1 Push the needle tip in and out of the fabric, making a small stitch.

2 Go back to where the thread disappears into the fabric and push the needle in.

3 Do another stitch, coming out a bit further along.

4 Do the same with each stitch, going back to fill in the space left by the stitch before.

Tip!
Use a backstitch when you need a strong seam or **hem**.

9

Pillow Cover

Pillows make your room feel cozy, friendly, and comfy. Make tons and you can relax in a big pile of them! Cotton, velvet, fake fur, or fleece fabric make good pillow covers.

Get the Gear!

- **Pillow form** or an old pillow to re-cover. It can be any size, but 18 in. (45 cm) square is a good size
- Fabric
- Scissors and tape measure
- Pins, needles, and thread
- About 12 in. (30 cm) of ribbon if you want a removable cover

1 Measure your pillow and cut a piece of fabric that's the same length and twice as wide as your pillow, plus an extra 1¼ in. (3 cm) all around.

1¼ in. (3 cm)

18 in. (45 cm)

18 in. (45 cm)

2 Fold the fabric in half "right sides together," which means that the patterned or "best" sides are face to face. Then pin the fabric together along the top and bottom, 1¼ in. (3 cm) in from the edge.

3 Now backstitch (see page 9) ¼ in. (0.5 cm) from the edge on the top and bottom, removing the pins as you go. At the end of each side, knot the thread and snip it off.

4 Fold the **raw edge** of the opening over twice to make a hem (neat edge). Pin along it, then sew all the way around using backstitch. Remove the pins. Remember, you don't want to sew it shut because the pillow needs to go inside!

Tip!
Ironing the hem flat will give a sharper edge and make it easier to sew. You should ask an adult to help you.

5 Turn the cover right side out. If you want a removable cover, sew two 6 in. (15 cm) pieces of ribbon to the opening using backstitch, so that you can tie the cover closed once the pillow is inside. If not, just insert the pillow and then sew the opening shut using a **whip stitch** (see box below).

How to Do a Whip Stitch

1 Thread your needle and knot the long end of the thread.

2 Push the needle tip through both fabrics and pull towards you over the top, making a stitch that pulls the two edges together.

3 Move the needle along slightly and do the same again. Keep stitching like this all the way along, then knot the thread and snip it off.

Decorated Pillow

Once you can make a basic pillow cover, get creative with different decorative designs. These work best on plain, flat fabrics.

Get the Gear!

- Pillow form or old pillow and fabric to cover it, as on page 10
- About 12 in. (30 cm) of ribbon
- Scissors and tape measure
- Pins, needles, and thread
- Buttons, beads, yarn or embroidery thread, scraps of felt or fleece fabric

1 Spread out your fabric. Choose which half will be the top, and use pins to mark where you want your design. It's easiest to add the design before putting the cover on the pillow. Three things to try are on page 13.

Tip!
Make a fluffy fake fur pillow into a bedroom monster by sewing on toy eyes (you can buy them at craft shops).

2 When you have added the design, sew the pillow cover together as on pages 10–11.

Line Art

Use brightly colored yarn or embroidery thread and a large needle. Knot the thread, and sew in from the back of the fabric. Then stitch a line of backstitch (see page 9) in the shape of a picture or pattern. You could even spell out words.

Buttons and Beads

Sew on small buttons or beads (see box below) to make a pattern or a shape such as a flower or face.

Appliqué

Appliqué means "applying" a fabric picture to something. Cut out a felt or fleece shape, such as a heart or animal. Pin it onto your pillow fabric, then sew it on using a backstitch. You can sew beads or buttons on top too.

Sewing on Beads and Buttons

Thread a needle and knot the end of the thread. Sew through from the back or inside of the fabric, and push the needle through the holes in the button or bead. Then sew through to the back again. Repeat several times before knotting at the back.

Panel Curtain

A panel curtain is a long, flat curtain that hangs straight down over your window. A **sheer** panel lets in light, but keeps your room private.

Get the Gear!

- Large piece of light, non-stretchy fabric, such as cotton voile, silk, or muslin, a bit bigger than your window
- Tape measure and scissors
- Pins, needles, and thread
- Ribbon, bias tape, or string

1 First, measure the space you want your curtain to cover. This is probably slightly bigger than your window pane, overlapping the window frame. For the curtain, you need a piece of fabric this size, plus about 2 in. (4 cm) all round.

2 Lay the fabric flat, with the patterned or "right" side down. Fold the edge in 1 in. (2 cm); then fold over again to make a hem. Do the long sides first, then the ends, so that the corners are folded in neatly. Pin the hem in place all round the edge.

hem

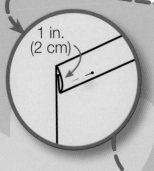

1 in. (2 cm)

14

3

Thread your needle and sew along the hem using a backstitch (see page 9) or a sewing machine if you have one. Take out the pins as you go.

4

Use a backstitch or whip stitch (see pages 9 and 11) to attach two loops of ribbon, bias tape, or string to the two top corners of the curtain.

5

Ask an adult to help you put two small hooks or nails into the window frame above the glass. Then you can hang the curtain up by the loops.

Tip!
Make sure the length of the loops and the positioning of the hooks match up, so that your curtain hangs in the right place.

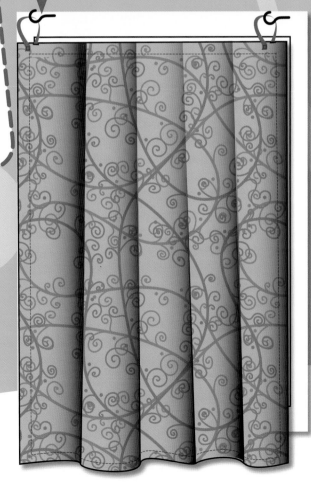

Handy Pocket

This handy pocket is a bit like a shelf, but you can sew it! Use it to hang a book by your bed, pencils by your desk, or a remote control wherever you need it.

Get the Gear!

- Quite strong, firm fabric such as thick cotton or canvas. For a book holder, use a piece about 20 in. (50 cm) square.
- About 8 in. (20 cm) of ribbon or bias tape
- Scissors and ruler
- Pins, needles, and thread

1 For a pocket to hold a notebook, cut four pieces of fabric in two sizes, like this.

9 in. (23 cm)

9 in. (23 cm)

7 in. (18 cm)

7 in. (18 cm)

2 Take the two larger pieces and put them "right sides together." Pin them together all around the edge.

3 Sew the fabric pieces together, about 1 in. (2 cm) in from the edge, using a backstitch (see page 9). Leave a gap at one end about 4 in. (10 cm) wide. Remove the pins.

4 in. (10 cm) gap

4 Turn the sewn piece right side out, pin the gap closed, and sew it shut using a backstitch. This is the back piece of the pocket.

Tip!
When turning right way out, use a ruler to push out the corners so they're nice and neat.

5 Do exactly the same thing with the smaller two pieces to make the front part of the pocket.

6 Now lay the front piece of the pocket on top of the back piece and pin it in place. Sew around the two sides and the bottom using backstitch.

7 Finally, sew two 4 in. (10 cm) lengths of ribbon or tape to the top corners to make hanging loops. Ask an adult to help you put up hooks or nails so you can hang your pocket wherever you want it.

Tip!
If you like, sew on buttons, beads, ribbons, or **sequins** as decoration.

Big Bedspread

Transform your boring bed! All you need is a colorful, soft, snuggly, funky bedspread.

Get the Gear!

- Big piece of fabric, at least 55 in. x 65 in. (140 cm x 160 cm)
- Ribbon (2 in. (5 cm) wide or more), long enough to go around your piece of fabric, plus 20 in. (50 cm)
- Scissors
- Pins
- Needle and thread, or a sewing machine

1

Spread out your fabric. Fold the ribbon in half lengthwise and start wrapping it around the edge of the fabric, pinning it in place as you go. Make sure the ribbon is folded neatly in half and the pins go through both sides of it.

2

At the corners, fold the ribbon over itself as you go around the corner, like this.

Tip!
Look for warm, cozy fabric, such as velvet, fleece, or fake fur with a fab animal print!

ribbon tucked in

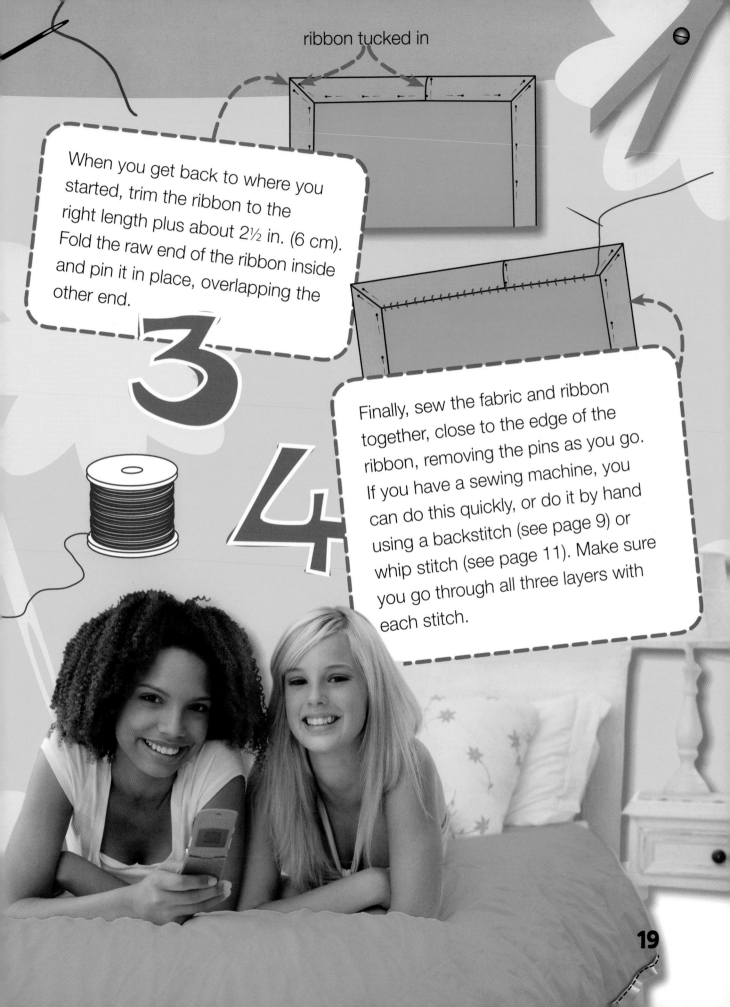

When you get back to where you started, trim the ribbon to the right length plus about 2½ in. (6 cm). Fold the raw end of the ribbon inside and pin it in place, overlapping the other end.

3

4

Finally, sew the fabric and ribbon together, close to the edge of the ribbon, removing the pins as you go. If you have a sewing machine, you can do this quickly, or do it by hand using a backstitch (see page 9) or whip stitch (see page 11). Make sure you go through all three layers with each stitch.

Patchwork Projects

Patchwork means sewing together pieces of fabric to make a big, flat pattern. It's perfect for using up fabric scraps and old clothes, and it looks amazing.

Get the Gear!

- Selection of different fabrics
- Sewing pins, needles, and thread
- Scissors and a tape measure or ruler

1 You need lots of different fabrics for your patches. A good patch size to start with is about 2½ in. (6 cm) square. Cut your fabric into 3 in. (8 cm) squares (this will allow for sewing the edges together).

3 in. (8 cm)

3 in. (8 cm)

2 To sew two squares together, lay them on top of each other right sides together, and pin them together along one side. Then backstitch (see page 9) along that side, about ¼ in. (1 cm) from the edge. Remove the pins.

3 Open out the squares, and pin and sew a new square to one of them, like this.

Tip!
Patchwork can be made up of any color combination you like—shades of one color, bright colors, pastels, or random patterns. Or you can use the patches to create a design of stripes or shapes as you go.

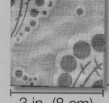

4 Keep adding more in the same way, until you have a strip of five or ten squares (or any number you like).

5 Repeat until you have several strips. If possible, iron them (with an adult to help you), or just smooth them out flat.

6 To sew two strips together, lay them down right sides together, neatly lined up, and pin and backstitch along ¼ in. (1 cm) from the edge. Keep adding more strips in the same way, and you'll end up with a whole patchwork panel.

Tip!
You can use patchwork to make pillows, bedspreads, or other projects in this book —or even for clothes! If you really enjoy patchwork, experiment with patches of different sizes and shapes. You can use rectangles, triangles, or hexagons.

Photo Frame

Put photos of family, friends, or pets in your room, and give them their own funky frames.

Get the Gear!

- Thick card stock, a little larger than your photo
- Ruler, pencil, and tape
- Craft knife or sharp scissors
- Paper scraps, craft glue and a brush, buttons, sequins, ribbons, stickers, or glitter

1 First, draw a frame in the middle of your card. This can be a basic square or rectangle, or other shapes, but the inside of the frame needs to be slightly smaller than your photo. Carefully cut out the frame, using a craft knife. Ask an adult to help you.

2 To decorate the frame, try these ideas:

Decoupage

Decoupage means gluing things onto paper to make a smooth, colorful covering. Use bits of torn-up tissue paper, old wrapping paper, magazine pictures, or old calendars. Paint craft glue onto the frame, stick down a piece of paper, and cover it with more glue. Keep going, overlapping the pieces until the frame is covered. Let dry.

Collage

Stick ribbons, buttons, sequins, or whatever you like onto your frame to decorate it. For example, you could cover it all over with little multicolored buttons. Or wrap ribbon all the way around it and glue it in place at the back.

Tip!
If you are going to use collage but not cover the entire frame, you might want to start with colored or sparkly card stock. Or you could glue colorful or interesting paper to your frame first.

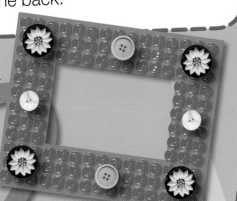

Fake It

Search for a photo of an old-fashioned, carved picture frame on the Internet, and print it out. Cut your card frame to the same size and glue the printed frame to it. Your fancy frame will make your photos look like works of fine art!

3 To attach the photo, put the frame face down, with your photo face down on top, making sure it overlaps the hole in the middle. Tape the back of the photo to the frame.

Tip!
To make a cardboard stand for your photo, just cut a strip of card stock, fold it and tape it to the back of the frame.

23

Writing on the Wall

Make a name sign to put on your door or decorate your wall.

Get the Gear!

- Ready-made craft letters from a craft shop, or thick cardboard for making your own
- Pencil
- Craft knife or sharp scissors
- Paper scraps, craft glue and brush, paint or markers, sequins, glitter, stick-on googly eyes

1 To make your own letters, use thick, white or light-colored cardboard. Draw your letters onto the cardboard, making them quite large (about 3 in. (8 cm) high or bigger). If you're not sure what style and shape to make them, look in books and magazines for letter shapes to copy.

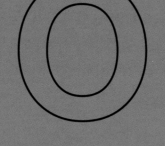

2 Cut out your letters carefully, using a scissors or craft knife (ask an adult to help).

3 Now decorate your letters! Look at the next page for some ideas.

24

Colors and Patterns

Use paints or markers to cover your letters with colors, stripes, spots, animal markings, or whatever you like. You can stick on googly eyes, sequins, or glitter too.

Decoupage

Cover your letters with paper scraps and craft glue, using the decoupage method shown on page 22.

Font Fun

Use a computer program such as Word to write big letters in interesting **fonts** and colors on the computer screen. Print them out, stick them onto the cardboard and carefully cut them out.

When your letters are finished, pin or tack them to your bedroom door or onto a wall (check with an adult first) to spell out your name or any words you like.

Wall Stencils

Jazz up your bedroom walls with patterns or pictures, using special decorating stencils. You can buy them, but it's more fun to make your own. (Check with a parent before decorating your bedroom walls, though!)

Get the Gear!

- Card stock
- Pencil
- Sharp scissors or a craft knife
- Removable painter's tape or masking tape
- Leftover wall paint or **acrylic paint**. Metallic paint would work well.
- Small decorating paintbrush or large art paintbrush
- Old clothes and newspapers

1 Draw your stencil designs onto card stock. They should be simple outline shapes, such as stars and moons, simple animals, hearts, arrows, or leaves.

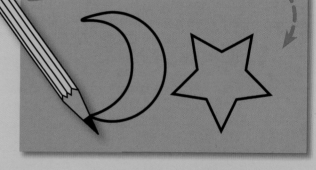

2 Carefully cut out the shapes, leaving the outline with a neat edge. This is easiest with a craft knife on top of cardboard such as the back of a pad of paper (ask an adult to help).

3

For the painting part, lay down plenty of old newspaper near the wall, and wear old clothes. Position each stencil on the wall where you want it, and attach with removable painter's tape.

Get a little paint on your brush and dab or wipe it to get rid of drips. Paint carefully inward, over the edge of the stencil toward the middle of the design.

4

5

Let dry and very carefully remove the stencil.

Recycled Waste Paper Basket

Every bedroom needs a waste paper basket—and this one is made from recycled waste paper!

Get the Gear!

- Lots of old newspapers
- Craft glue or tape
- Scissors

1 First make about 20 strips that your basket will be made from. Take a sheet of newspaper and fold it over and over to make a flat strip about 1¼ in. (3 cm) wide and 24 in. (60 cm) long. Use glue or tape to hold it in place.

2 Now to make your basket. Take six strips and lay them down together. Take another strip, and weave it over and under the six strips, so it ends up in the middle, like this.

3 Take the next strip, and do the same, but go under the strips you went over before, and over the strips you went under before, like this.

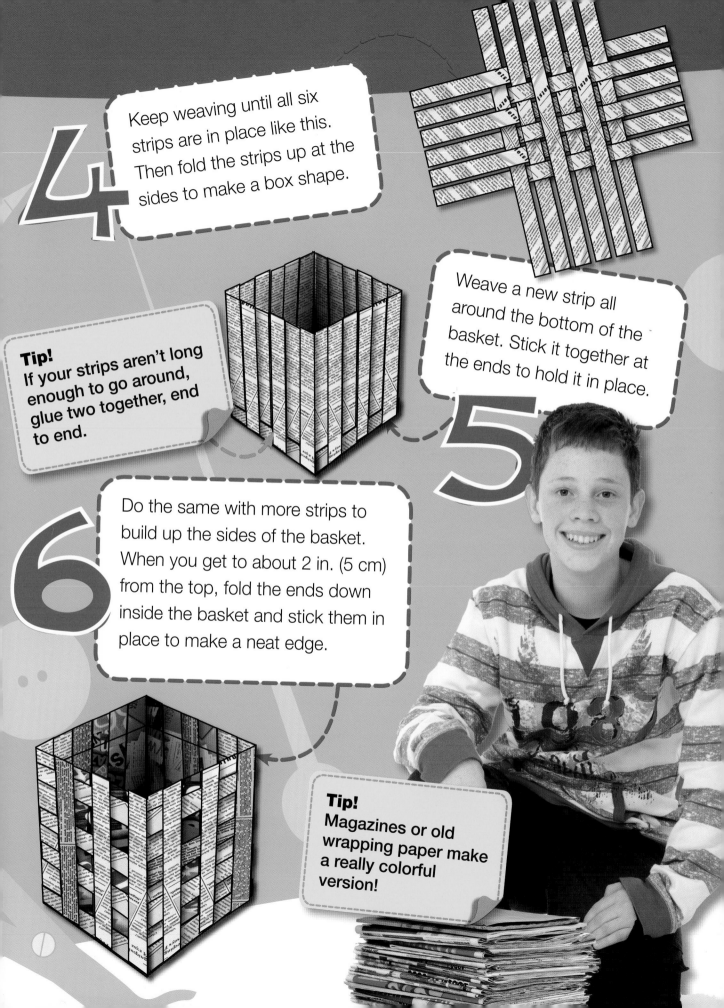

4 Keep weaving until all six strips are in place like this. Then fold the strips up at the sides to make a box shape.

Tip!
If your strips aren't long enough to go around, glue two together, end to end.

5 Weave a new strip all around the bottom of the basket. Stick it together at the ends to hold it in place.

6 Do the same with more strips to build up the sides of the basket. When you get to about 2 in. (5 cm) from the top, fold the ends down inside the basket and stick them in place to make a neat edge.

Tip!
Magazines or old wrapping paper make a really colorful version!

Equipment Tips

Here's a quick guide to finding the things you need for your bedroom makeover projects.

Buttons and beads
Find these at sewing shops, craft shops, discount stores, and special bead shops. You can also check thrift stores, rummage sales, and reuse buttons and beads from old clothes and jewelry.

Card stock and cardboard
Craft and hobby shops usually have several types of card stock. You can also reuse cardboard from packaging for some projects.

Craft knife
You can get a good, easy-to-use craft knife at a craft or hobby shop. Ask an adult to help you use it.

Craft letters
Some craft shops sell large wooden or cardboard letters.

Embroidery thread (also called floss)
This is often sold in sewing and craft shops or knitting shops, and comes in hundreds of colors. Look for good quality, cotton thread, which is easy to use and is washable.

Fabric
Fabric shops, craft shops, and some department stores sell new fabrics by the yard or meter. Check bargain bins for cheaper **remnants**. Ask friends and family if they have old clothes, linens, or curtains you could cut up and reuse.

Felt
Fabric shops, discount stores, and craft shops often have felt. You can buy small squares for crafts or by the yard for larger sewing projects.

Glue
Craft and hobby shops sell craft glue and white glue.

Needles
Find in sewing shops. Look for a variety pack with lots of different sizes.

Old clothes
As well as reusing your own old fabrics, ask family members for anything they don't want any more, and check out thrift stores and rummage sales.

Online
There are many fabric and craft shops on the Internet. You may find the following sites useful starting points:
www.fabric.com
www.amazon.com/Arts-Crafts-Sewing
www.moodfabrics.com

Paint, markers, and paintbrushes
Discount stores are best for these, if you don't have them around at home.

Pillow forms
Craft and hobby shops often have these.

Pins
Find at sewing shops. Longer pins with ball-shaped heads are the easiest to use.

Ribbons
Sewing and fabric shops usually sell ribbons and trimmings by the yard or meter.

Scissors
The sharper your scissors, the easier they are to work with, but take care when using them.

Sequins
You can often find these at craft and hobby shops.

Sewing machines

This book doesn't show you how to use a sewing machine, but if you have one, you can use it for most of the projects. Follow the machine's instructions, and get an adult to help you. If you want to buy a sewing machine, try a discount store or sewing shop.

Stencils

You can get ready-made wall stencils at hobby and craft shops.

Thread

Find at sewing shops. Use extra-strong thread for sewing through heavy fabrics.

Glossary

acrylic paint
A type of hardwearing, quick-drying paint.

appliqué
A technique used to decorate clothing or other fabric items by attaching fabric shapes.

backstitch
A strong sewing stitch that goes over each part of the fabric twice.

bias tape
Strong, ribbon-like tape made of woven fabric.

bunting
Strings of colorful flags.

decoupage
Covering something with glued-on paper scraps.

embroidery
Using colored thread to sew designs on fabric.

font
A style of lettering.

gather
To pull fabric together into a bundle or crinkle using a line of stitching.

hem
The edge of a piece of fabric, folded over and sewn in place to stop it from unravelling.

pillow form
The inside part of a pillow.

raw edge
The unfinished or cut edge of a piece of fabric.

remnants
Leftover pieces of fabric.

running stitch
A simple, in-and-out sewing stitch.

sequins
Little shiny or metallic discs with a hole in the middle.

sheer
Very thin, or partly see-through.

stencil
A cut-out shape for coloring or painting through.

whip stitch
A looping sewing stitch for sewing along edges.

·Index